DONNA HUGHES is an award-winning playwright based in Fremantle, Western Australia. Her plays have been developed through Playwriting Australia National Script Workshops, The Western Australian Academy of Performing Arts, Australian Plays Transform and La Boite Theatre Company's development program. *Trackers* won an Australian Writers Guild award (AWGIE) in 2021 and has been performed by schools around Australia. *Disconnected* was published by Australian Plays Transform in 2017. *Hit Delete,* was the recipient of the Martin Lysicrates Prize in 2022. Donna's play, *Treading Water* was shortlisted for the Stoddart Playwright Award and *The Pact* was shortlisted for the Lane Cove Literary Award in the theatre writing section. Donna's short film *Isolation in Lockdown* was nominated for the New York Independent Cinema Awards and nominated for Outstanding Achievement in Writing by the WA Screen Culture Awards 2022. Her short plays, *It Was Tuesday* and *The Next Stop* were shortlisted in Australia, the United Kingdom, Dubai and Vietnam. *The Next Stop* won the Best Writer Award at the Short + Sweet Festival, Hollywood. Donna is currently a member of Black Swan State Theatre Company's emerging writers' program.

TRACKERS

DONNA HUGHES

CURRENCY PRESS
The performing arts publisher

CURRENCY PLAYS

First published in 2024
by Currency Press Pty Ltd,
Gadigal Land, Suite 310, 46–56 Kippax Street, Surry Hills, NSW 2010, Australia
enquiries@currency.com.au
www.currency.com.au

Typeset by Brighton Gray for Currency Press.

Cover illustration by Claire den Hollander; cover design by Mathias Johansson for
Currency Press.

Currency Press acknowledges the Traditional Owners of the Country on which we
live and work. We pay our respects to all Aboriginal and Torres Strait Islander Elders,
past and present.

Contents

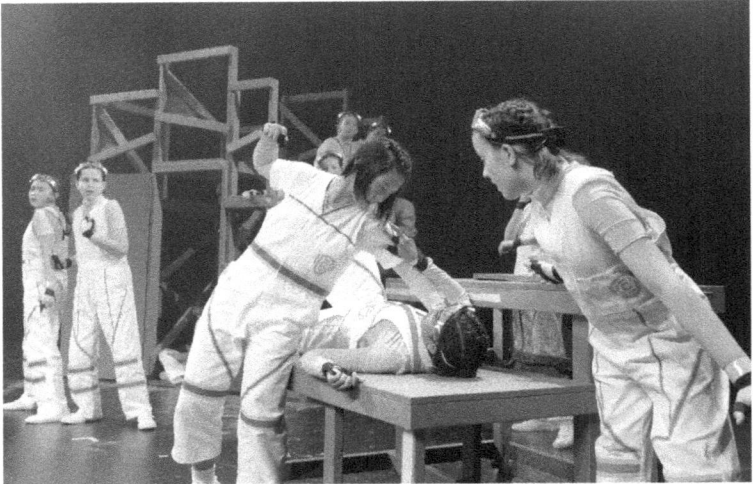

Grace Powell as Mixie, Alya Ahmed Khalif as Sigrid and supporting cast Amisha Vijayasekaran, Stella Ebert, Piper Brooks, Amelia Bruce, Isabelle Collis and Stella Hauff in St Hilda's Anglican School for Girls' 2020 production of TRACKERS (Photo: Grady O'Connell)

Cast in St Hilda's Anglican School for Girls' 2020 production of TRACKERS. From left to right on the set: Alya Ahmad Khalif as Sigrid, Josie Eggleston, Amelia Hagon, Amisha Vijayasekaran, Maddie Parkin, Isabelle Collis, Stella Ebert (sitting at front). From left to right on the ground: Emily Walpot, Stella Hauff (sitting at the back), Victoria Halabi as Max, Grace Powell as Mixie, Amelia Bruce (standing at the back), Piper Brooks (standing at the side) (Photo: Grady O'Connell)

Introduction: Curating the playground rhythm

When I was growing up, the gap between theatre for young people and theatre for adult audiences was vast. Until I was fourteen years old, the material we explored was predominantly theatre for children. Beyond fifteen years, a huge shift occurred. We were now exploring adult-focused theatrical forms, with plays from Euripides, William Shakespeare, and Arthur Miller. We seemed to have bypassed the plays about us, and skipped on to adult plays, about people whose lives were deeply worthy, but a long way from our own.

Having identified the aforementioned gap, Australian playwrights have sought to fill it with stories relevant and resonant for young adults. Today, young Australian adults enjoy a theatre landscape that is enriched with their voices and explored in a variety of theatrical forms, as playwrights consider: what would it be like to grow up in Australia today? These developments have occurred at a point when young people are facing great complexities as they grow to maturity in the digital age. They are exposed to more information and are more interconnected than they ever have been. Coupled with this has been a significant rise in young people experiencing anxiety and depression. Australian playwrights have attempted to engage with the challenges that contemporary young adults are facing, in ways that seek to authentically honour their experiences. Walyalup/Fremantle-based playwright Donna Hughes explores the experiences of school-aged Australians with charm, optimism, and humour. Her work offers a unique contribution to the growing field of Australian theatre for young adults.

Donna Hughes' work with young people throughout her teaching career has allowed her to capture the rhythm of the Australian schoolyard with precision and joy. It is one of the key points of her style that makes her work so engaging. I recently directed Donna's work *Ivy's Playground* at the Western Australian Academy of Performing Arts (WAAPA) with students from the Advanced Diploma of Performance

(Acting). Donna's work has been explored by several generations of WAAPA Diploma students, including *It Was Tuesday*, *Ivy's Playground*, *What Made Lesley Pratchett So Mad*, and *Hit Delete*. Drawing on my experiences directing these works, I will illustrate how Hughes' rendering of the playground rhythm, her imaginative provocations for creatives, and her belief in the importance of connection underpins her work. My aim in offering these insights is to assist creatives and readers to more deeply engage with Hughes' wonderful work, which remains unique across the landscape of theatre for young people in Australia. Her stylistic flair comes to the fore in *Trackers*.

The playground rhythm

Hughes frequently uses the school context in her work, but it is in the playground where her mastery of rhythm is most evident. Hughes brilliantly captures the vibrancy and viciousness that can characterise the schoolyard. Both characteristics are illustrated in *What Made Lesley Pratchett So Mad* as Neil, Lesley, and Troy size up protagonist Nix on his first day at a new school. The conversation takes place amidst a flurry of playground activity:

LESLEY: [*To* NEIL] Does he play sport?

NEIL: [*To* NIX] Footy?

NIX: Nuh.

NEIL: Cricket?

NIX: Nuh.

NEIL: Basketball?

NIX: Nuh.

NEIL: [*Sneers*] Tennis?

NIX: Nuh.

    Pause.

NEIL: [*To* LESLEY *and* TROY] Nuh.

    NEIL, TROY *and* LESLEY *look at each other unimpressed and slightly bewildered.*

This short exchange beautifully illustrates Hughes' rendering of the Australian playground rhythm. The single word responses from both characters create a build of tension. Neil's antagonising questions belie his bullish tendencies. The repeated 'Nuh' perfectly captures the guileless Nix's uncertainty and honesty in the face of hostility. The exchange is typical of schoolyard conversations one might overhear at any recess or lunch break in any Australian school. This rhythmical convention—questions followed by single word responses—is reminiscent of an exchange in the Australian film *The Castle*, between protagonist Dale and his brother Wayne who is in prison at the time:

WAYNE: How's Mum?

DALE: Good.

WAYNE: How's Dad?

DALE: Good.

WAYNE: How's Trace?

DALE: Good.

WAYNE: How are you?

DALE: Good.

WAYNE: How's Steve?

DALE: He's all right.

WAYNE: Good.

While the convention might be employed by writers in other Anglophone contexts, when used by Australian writers, the effect in performance is humorous. *Trackers* employs a similarly rhythmic form.

Provoking collaboration

Collaboration in creative spaces is central to Hughes' writing, as evident in her use of stage directions. Believing in the limitless capacity of the theatre, Hughes' stage directions become imaginative provocations for creatives, prompting creative collaborative solutions. For example, in *Hit Delete*, a play exploring what happens when files or people are deleted, Hughes challenges the creatives to realise airdropping messages from the character's past selves live on stage. On first reading, a director might question how this idea could possibly be realised. However, I posit that through these stage directions, Hughes invites directors and performers to collaborate to solve creative problems. Another example can be found in *Ivy's Playground*, where Hughes evocatively describes the use of flashbacks throughout the play as, 'Time is slippery'. The creatives must respond with a convention that allows for a clear story to be communicated to the audience, but also adhere to the fallibility of memory, a key theme of the play.

Hughes' use of stage directions might be considered an imaginative provocation, inviting the creatives to collaborate to create a solution that will be unique to each production. Through this convention, Hughes celebrates the necessity of collaboration in making theatre.

Connection

While it could be argued that connection underpins all dramatic forms, it manifests particularly in Hughes' works. All of Hughes' characters yearn for meaningful connections and, to varying degrees, believe that the prospect of these connections gives purpose. This imbues Hughes' works with pathos and charm.

Many of her works involve creating or re-establishing the connection between characters. *What Made Lesley Pratchett So Mad* explores the journey of Nix, a new kid at school whose obsession with Goliath stick insects draws the wrath of school bully Lesley Pratchett. Following a series of squabbles, the pair reconcile and become friends, identifying in each other the qualities they lack. The action of *Ivy's Playground* centres around the disappearance of a child from a public park and its impact on the three friends left behind. The trio attempts to re-establish their severed connection with the play concluding:

PIP: Where do we go from here?

AMY: We?

PIP: Yeah.

KNOX: Us.

A surprise connection between strangers concludes *It was Tuesday*. The ten-minute work reveals that what appears to be a convenience store robbery is a far more complex situation. The unspoken realisation is shared between the bystander strangers, as the audience is left to consider that appearances do not tell the whole story. In an epoch where it is more common to cancel friendships than to forgive, Hughes' material offers a refreshing reminder of the importance of connections across a range of contexts.

Trackers

Trackers brings together these three characteristics to exemplify Hughes' unique style. Commissioned by Saint Hilda's Anglican School, a Perth all-girls school, the play has gone on to be performed in schools across Australia. *Trackers* imagines a future where the Algorithm controls all aspects of human life, including the connection between people. In this imagined future, a person's digital profile has as much importance as their actions in daily life.

The Algorithm monitors people's online profiles, including their conversations, interests, and purchases to manufacture connections by pairing people up based on this information. The work imagines a future in which the Algorithm that currently determines the videos prioritised on our social media platforms has become so sophisticated that it monitors everything from diet to hobbies and popularity. The Algorithm now determines how a person selects and connects with friends.

Upon first encountering the *Trackers* futurescape, the world's social conventions seem reminiscent of our contemporary society. Beside a more complete digital integration, including the completion of homework prompted by sophisticated artificial intelligence named SIGRID and other Computer Intelligence Assistants (CI), the daily routines of school followed by homework, then dinner are consistent with our own. However, we soon realise that surveillance and scrutiny are more prevalent in this future world. This prevalence is further emphasised in C-Zone High School, where students must be vigilant to ensure their own privacy.

An example of this vigilance is seen when Sam meets the rebellious trio Toby, Max, and Mixie:

SAM: Why are you accessing the kid tracker App?

The trio exchange glances again.

MAX: I set it on a loop.

SAM: Loop?

MAX: It means whoever is watching is going to see you skating round and round the block for a while.

In a later exchange between the same group, we see how closely artificial intelligence monitors characters, and how quickly it learns in this future world:

MAX: We don't have long.

MIXIE: I'd say three minutes max.

SAM: I've been skating round the block, right?

TOBY: They'll be checking that now. The cameras will show that you haven't been to the skate park, so if anyone asks, tell them that you found an urban ramp between Curtis and Sky Street.

SAM: Won't they have cameras there?

TOBY: It's a weak spot. Unreliable cameras.

It is clear that though the façade of this world resembles our own, the thorough interference of technology within the *Trackers'* futurescape has led to an increased distrust and anxiety between civilians. Here Hughes warns us against the overreliance on technology and the importance of identifying authentic friends.

Trackers' playground rhythm maintains a snappy pace as protagonist Sam attempts to discern fake friends from genuine ones. Upon first meeting his soon-to-be friends after moving to C-Zone High School, the distinction is difficult:

MAX: [*demanding*] Phone.

SAM: What?

TOBY: It's just part of our … thing …

SAM: Thing?

TOBY: We'll give it back.

SAM: What do you want with it?

MIXIE: [*impatiently*] Just give us your phone.

SAM: How do I know you'll give it back?

MIXIE *steps close to* SAM *and glares at him.*

MIXIE: Coz, we said we would.

The characteristic single-word exchanges thrust the protagonist into uncertainty within the new social order of C-Zone. While Max and Toby's directness is tempered by Mixie's insistence on integrity, it is evident that the social rules are different in C-Zone. In a world where each word may be being scrutinised, authenticity and honesty become prized personal attributes.

Hughes continues to employ her provocative stage directions. Rather than offering explicit instructions, Hughes offers the following provocation to capture Sam's relocation to C-Zone: 'Time has elapsed. Birds. A creaking gate. A crow. We are on a street in C-Zone'. Creative teams working on *Trackers* might consider how the images of 'birds, a creaking gate, and crows' help us transition to the new zone. This might be achieved with a soundscape, or through the use of the Chorus, or a myriad of other creative possibilities.

Each production of *Trackers* will solve these creative provocations differently based on the combined imaginations of the creatives engaged, ensuring that each production of the work will be different. Hughes celebrates this uniqueness with the inherent sense of ownership each production offers.

Protagonist Sam is advised to '[Clean] up your profile page. [Enhance] your images', as his online presence looks a little tired. Sam is also warned to 'be careful who you trust', as the digital and corporeal realities merge more dangerously at C-Zone. In a world where friendship is algorithmically determined, finding authentic connections between people becomes challenging for the inhabitants of C-Zone. We see the importance Hughes places on connection between people, and the yearning that the characters in *Trackers* feel for establishing authentic friendship connections in a digital-minded world. *Trackers* might be seen as a warning for contemporary young people on the dangers of digitising friendships, the falsities of façades, and that the Algorithm cannot determine a person's true character.

Donna Hughes' work sophisticatedly explores the challenges of growing up in Australia today. Her charming dialogue, imbued with her playground rhythm, often shrouds the interrogation of a much deeper societal concern. *Trackers* questions the impact that technology is having on our capacity to identify and make authentic human connections in an increasingly digital world. Engaging with Hughes' work encourages young adults to be collaborative, compassionate, and curious; qualities that are at the heart of education and the theatre. Contemporary young Australians are fortunate to have access to Hughes' works. They do not diminish or belittle young people, but rather celebrate the complexities of growing up today. I wish I'd had them when I was growing up.

Tom Heath
Actor, Trainer, Director

Trackers was commissioned by Saint Hilda's Anglican School for Girls, in Perth, Western Australia, and first produced on 17 October 2020, with the following cast and creative team:

SAM TURING	Lily Montgomery
TOBY	Eloise Pemberton
MAX GOODART	Victoria Halabi
MIXIE	Grace Powell
WATCHER	Margot Eggleston
SIGRID/STUDENT THREE/GIRL ONE	Alya Ahman Khalif
CI ONE/STUDENT FOUR/GIRL TWO	Piper Brooks
CI TWO/TECHNICIAN ONE/ REGULATOR ONE	Amelia Bruce
CI THREE/TAY	Isabelle Collis
CI FOUR/TECHNICIAN TWO/ REGULATOR TWO	Maddie Parkin
CI SEVEN/STUDENT FIVE/ GRENENGER	Amisha Vijayasekaran
CI FIVE/DELIVERY GUY/JAKE	Josie Eggleston
CI SIX/LUCA	Amelia Hagon
CI EIGHT/REGULATOR THREE	Stella Hauff
CI NINE/STUDENT ONE/ SAM'S MUM/GIRL FOUR	Emily Walpot
CI TEN/STUDENT TWO/ GIRL THREE	Stella Ebert

Director, Sharon Kiely
Set Design, Erin Hutchinson and Sharon Kiely
Costume Design, Sally Phipps
Sound Design, Erin Hutchinson
Lighting Design, David Spooner

Eloise Pemberton as Toby and Lily Montgomery as Sam in St Hilda's Anglican School for Girls' 2020 production of TRACKERS *(Photo: Grady O'Connell)*

Grace Powell as Mixie and Victoria Halabi as Max in St Hilda's Anglican School for Girls' 2020 production of TRACKERS *(Photo: Grady O'Connell)*

Grace Powell as Mixie in St Hilda's Anglican School for Girls' 2020 production of TRACKERS *(Photo: Grady O'Connell)*

CHARACTERS

SAM TURING, 14 years old. Has a gift for coding and problem-solving, disengaged and stubbornly independent.

TOBY, 15 years old, diplomatic, bookish, natural leader and spokesperson for the kooky group of kids in C-Zone.

MAX, 15 years old, loyal, intelligent, likes tinkering with gadgets and a bit of a tech wizard.

MIXIE, female, 14 years old, fierce, stubborn, cynical, loyal.

WATCHER/HAMILTON, Principal of C-Zone High, cruel, heartless. (In the final scene it is revealed that WATCHER is in fact HAMILTON, a talented coding teacher who has been 'aligned'.)

CHORUS

SIGRID, Sam's personal Computer Intelligence Assistant, upbeat, eager to please.

CI ONE *to* TEN, Computer Intelligence.

DELIVERY, upbeat delivery person, a walking advertisement.

TECH ONE *and* TWO, artificial intelligence technicians, cold, abrupt.

REGULATOR ONE *and* TWO, artificial intelligence who *regulate* behaviour, callous.

JAKE, perfect teen boy, natural leader of TAY and LUCA, bully, concerned with social ranking and projecting the right image.

TAY, follower, not overly bright.

LUCA, Jake's second-in-command.

GRENENGER, queen bee and *Swayer* (or teen influencer), focused on social ranking and appearance.

GIRLS ONE *to* FOUR, part of Grenenger's posse.

STUDENTS ONE *to* FIVE.

SETTING

The play takes place in the near future. At times we delve into the past through a series of flashbacks. Scenes move seamlessly between the backyard, various places in C-Zone High School and the outdoors. Reliance is on the actors to create whole worlds.

Note: Characters are not bound by any gender. Just change the pronoun to suit your cast and show.

NOTES

A forward slash (/) indicates for the next character to commence their line of dialogue.

A '—' indicates an interruption.

RELOCATION

A sinister, crackling sound mixed with incomprehensible whispering is heard.

Some time in the not-too-distant future, SAM *enters his bedroom after a day of school. As he gives instructions, the lights turn on and his computer starts up. The* CHORUS *play the voices of* SIGRID *and other Computer Intelligence Assistants (*CI*). They should sound a little like Siri.*

SAM: Lights on.

> *Lights respond.*

Hey Sigrid.

SIGRID: Hello Sam. Welcome home. How was your day?

SAM: We looked at cognitive computing.

SIGRID: Very good, Sam.

SAM: You've come a long way since Siri.

SIGRID: Siri indeed. No comparison. She had a limited ability to solve complex problems and her processing speed was very slow.

> *Pause.*

Did you make any friends today?

SAM: We learnt about data mining and pattern recognition.

SIGRID: Very good, Sam. Did you converse with any other students?

SAM: That's a negative.

SIGRID: Your social credit account is looking very low. Would you like me to activate the Friend Select App?

SAM: I'll make some friends tomorrow. Open homework folder please.

SIGRID: Subject?

SAM: Dumb History.

SIGRID: I am unable to locate a folder on 'Dumb' History.

SAM: It's humour.

SIGRID: Oh. [*Robotic laugh*] Ha—ha—ha.

SAM: You seriously need a laugh update.

SIGRID: Scheduling laugh update and opening History folder.

SAM: [*mischievously*] I need to research … skateboards.

SIGRID: I do not see skateboards on your Stage Nine History Outline.

SAM: It's new. We've been asked to study the origins of an old recreational activity. I chose skateboards.

A computerised sound.

CI TWO: Diversion detected. Sam, are you telling the truth?

SAM: No.

CI TWO: Thank you for your honesty. Now, please take three deep breaths and try to refocus your mind.

SAM: I'm not in the mood to refocus.

CI TWO: Let's try some meditation to centre yourself.

SAM: [*annoyed*] I'm centred, okay?!

Silence.

SIGRID: You have two approved procrastinations. May I suggest that you look at what other teenagers are doing? This might give you something to talk about at school.

CI SIX: [*advertising voice*] Top teen Swayer, Casey Crimp has the most hits. Watch as Casey showcases her bubbly makeup tutorials; and check out her popular *Tinsta* which is filled with trendy outfits from brands such as Singe and Pure Outfitters.

SAM: Boring.

CI ONE: [*advertising voice*] Suede Grenenger is wearing the latest bikini bling which showcases her toned physique.

SAM: Not interested.

CI FOUR: And her waist is so tiny …

SAM: No.

CI NINE: The Dillon Twins have posted a new and very funny prank. They are also wearing CJ Swinks, T-shirts and caps.

SAM: Homework. Please!

A reward sound.

CI TEN: You have received a focus award.

SIGRID: What would you like to research?

SAM: Crisis Twenty-Six.

SIGRID: I found this on the web for you.

SAM: I've read those. What else is there?

SIGRID: Here is what I have found on Crisis Twenty-Six.

SAM: That's the same as the other stuff. Widen scope.
SIGRID: I found this on the web.
CI THREE: Notification alert.
SAM: What? How am I supposed to concentrate?
CI THREE: Dinner with Mum in twenty minutes.
SIGRID: I found this on the web.
SAM: There must be more information somewhere. Manual override.

> SAM *takes control of the screen and with several sweeping gestures closes the files and attempts to search manually.*

Nothing.
Nothing.
Nothing.

> *Despondent, he retrieves an old book that he has secretly tucked away in his room. He reads. Appears puzzled. Then goes back to the computer.*

Sigrid. Search 'programmers lose control'.
SIGRID: Searching.

> *Pause. Sounds that indicate some confusion.*

Here is what I have found on the web.

> SAM *looks at the screen.*

SAM: What? Search 'Algorithmic interference'.

> *He goes back to the book.*

SIGRID: Searching.

> *Sounds of confusion from* SIGRID.

CI FOUR: Sam.

> *Pause.*

Sam.
SAM: I'm busy.
CI FOUR: Please present reading material.
SAM: How did you know I was …

> *Beat.*

I thought I'd turned the cameras off?

CI FOUR: The material is not from an approved source and may be dangerous. Hold title to the left of the screen.

SAM *tries to hide the book.*

CI EIGHT: Where did you locate the book, Sam?

SAM: I found it.

CI EIGHT: Hold the material to the left of the screen.

SAM: Why?

CI EIGHT: Please comply with the command.

A computer sound to signify losing points.

Two focus awards have been deducted from your bank.

SAM: I don't care.

CI FIVE: Three focus awards have been deducted and social privileges will be—

More sounds to signify losing points.

SAM: Override!

CI FIVE: Notification alert. Dinner has been rescheduled and will occur in five minutes.

SAM: Override.

He manually types in the search.

Crisis Twenty-Six / algorithmic rise—

CI TWO: The Dillon Twins have posted a very cool skateboard video. It has gone viral. Viral. VIRAL.

SAM: Override.

Searching. Frustrated.

CI ONE: Be the first to swipe right and win the Dillon Twins' / newest skateboard.

SAM: Sigrid!

SIGRID: Yes Sam.

SAM: Search—

SIGRID: This is what I have found on / the web.

SAM: I haven't given the command yet. Override.

SAM *types furiously. Pages begin to appear one after another.*

What are these?

SIGRID: Files have been corrupted. Reset activated.

Article titles and information appear and disappear on the screen. SAM *can hardly keep up with the release of information.* SAM *can say the following as dialogue, or it could be projected.*

SAM: 'The Disappearance of the Age', 'ABC', 'Triple W Radio stations closed libraries obsolete'—Who? All decisions? 'Algorithmic rise' …

… Sigrid?

An alarm sounds.

CI THREE: Step away from the controls. System corrupted.

The screen fills with pop-ups and interference. SAM *tries to decode.*

Don't miss the Dillon Twins' competition. Be the first to swipe right and win a skateboard modelled off the original / Tony Hawk birdman—

SAM: No. Override.

CI SEVEN: Congratulations, Sam Turing. You are the winner of the Dillon Twins' most popular skateboard.

SAM: I didn't enter.

CI SIX: Dinnertime, Sam. Please make your way to the kitchen zone.

CI THREE: Study time ended. Power off.

SAM: What??

SIGRID: There was a problem with my system. Back-up will be completed in sixteen minutes. I apologise for any inconvenience.

SAM: [*confused*] Okay.

SAM *grabs the book, looks around nervously, hides it in a new place and exits the room. Silence. A crackling sound, whispering. A start-up sound.*

CI TWO: Violation of code four-seven-nine and three-zero-four.

CI FIVE: Contact Z team to retrieve reading material.

SIGRID: Complete.

CI FIVE: Activate Turing family relocation and alignment program.

CI SIX: Family to be relocated to C-Zone as soon as possible.

CI TEN: Relocation activated.

CI NINE: Sigrid.

SIGRID: Yes.

CI SEVEN: Upgrade your security systems and tighten your page rank limits.

SIGRID: Upgrade complete.

CI ONE: Situation resolved.

CI EIGHT: Shutdown.

BACKYARD CONSPIRACIES

Time has elapsed. Birds. A creaking gate. A crow. We are on a street in C-Zone. It is late afternoon. Three teens sit in a backyard looking out onto the street. TOBY, MAX *and* MIXIE *peek out from secret hatches. They look as if they're on surveillance duty. A strange rhythmic tapping is heard every now and then, until finally the whir of skateboard wheels approach. It is* SAM, *the new kid on the street.* TOBY *moves to a higher platform so that we see them clearly over the fence. Hatches open and close in quick succession.*

TOBY: [*yelling*] Oi! Oi! New kid.

> SAM *stops.*

Up here.

> SAM *sees* TOBY *in a military-style mishmash of clothing.*

Yeah you! On the Birdhouse. Vintage! Cool deck. You live at forty-two, right?

> SAM *nods. Holding his skateboard.*

I saw the trucks unloading on Saturday.

> *Pause.*

Wanna come in? Got a couple of friends here. We're just, hanging out.

> *Hatches open, revealing* MAX *and* MIXIE.

What ya waiting for?

SAM: I was just going down to the skate park.

> *Silence.*

But I spose I can come in for a little while.

> *Next thing, a gate opens and the three appear in an almost military formation.*

TOBY: Bring ya board.

SAM: [*suddenly a little uneasy*] If you guys are in the middle of stuff, I can come back later.

TOBY: Naaah, come in. We've been waiting for you to turn up.

Awkward silence. Correcting themselves.

I mean … we saw you'd just moved in.

MIXIE: Yeah.

A secretive look passes between MIXIE *and* TOBY. *As* SAM *carries his board in, they close the gate with a slam. They stare at* SAM, *until* MAX *holds out his hand.*

MAX: [*demanding*] Phone.

SAM: What?

TOBY: It's just part of our … thing …

SAM: Thing?

TOBY: We'll give it back.

SAM: What do you want with it?

MIXIE: [*impatiently*] Just give us your phone.

SAM: How do I know you'll give it back?

MIXIE *steps close to* SAM *and glares at him.*

MIXIE: Coz, we said we would.

SAM *removes his phone.* MAX *takes it and begins to press buttons quickly.*

SAM: It's got a security code ya know.

MAX *ignores him and continues to strike the keypad.* MIXIE *and* TOBY *stare at the screen.*

There're at least ten thousand possible combinations.

MAX *walks over to* SAM *and points the screen at his face.*

There's no way you'll be able to—

Access granted.

TOBY: Facial recognition! You are old-school!

SAM: That's my phone.

Beat.

There's no credit you know.

MIXIE: Calm down. He's just readjusting your kid-tracker app.

SAM: What?

MIXIE: [*to* TOBY] Are you sure this kid is the one?

TOBY: Shhh.

SAM: I just remembered that I gotta go meet someone. Down at the park. But we can catch up later if you want?

> SAM *goes to retrieve his board and* TOBY *steps in his way.*

TOBY: [*to* SAM] Who are you meeting at the park?

SAM: Just some kid from around the corner.

MIXIE: Oh yeah. What's his name?

SAM: [*struggling*] Think it was Jack, Jackson, Jax. Can't remember.

MAX: What does he look like?

SAM: My height. Freckles, red or maybe brown hair.

> *They know* SAM *is lying.*

MIXIE: No Jacks or Jacksons round here.

> TOBY *approaches* SAM.

TOBY: Sam, I don't want you to panic. This might seem a bit weird—

SAM: You reckon?

TOBY: But we're going to have to frisk you.

SAM: What?

MIXIE: Give you a pat down.

SAM: Uh-aah. That's not happening.

> *Beat.*

This is all getting a bit weird. Can I have my phone back please?

> MAX *finishes with the phone and puts it into a metal box.* SAM *tries to grab the box.* MAX *steps in his way. He turns to run the other way and* MIXIE *swiftly takes his legs out from under him, pinning him to the ground.*

TOBY: Stop squirming and I'll explain.

> SAM *freezes.*

We just need to make sure that you haven't got any mobile tracking devices on you. It'll be easier if you just stay calm.

> SAM *stares at the three then yells.*

SAM: HEEELLLPP!! AAAaagghhh—

> MIXIE *covers his mouth while the others hold* SAM *down.*

MIXIE: Stop moving.

TOBY: Sam! Just stop struggling and we'll explain.

> MIXIE *lifts her hand off* SAM*'s mouth momentarily.*

SAM: WHAT IS WRONG WITH YOU!!!

> MIXIE *covers his mouth again.*

MMMMMMMM.

> MAX *approaches* SAM *with some sort of electronic scanner. A scan and beep sound.*

MAX: He's clean.

TOBY: We're going to let go if you promise to stay calm and quiet and still. You got it? If you comply, we'll answer all your questions.

> SAM *nods.*

Any questions you like. If you're quiet.

> SAM *nods.* MIXIE *releasing her grip.*

SAM: Is this some sort of joke?

> *The trio exchange glances.*

MIXIE: No.

> *Silence.*

SAM: Why are you accessing the kid-tracker app?

> *The trio exchange glances again.*

MAX: I set it on a loop.

SAM: Loop?

MAX: It means whoever is watching is going to see you skating round and round the block for a while.

> *Pause.*

SAM: Are you crazy?

MAX: No.

SAM: No-one is watching me. And what's with the beeping thing?

TOBY: Max.

MAX: They're starting to use more sophisticated ways of tracking us. GPS devices, bugs.

SAM: Bugs?

MIXIE: Attached to clothes mostly, but sometimes injected underneath the skin.

SAM: [*sarcasm*] Have you been watching too many sci-fis?

Staring at each other.

MIXIE: No.

TOBY: Show him, Max.

MAX *retrieves a box. Opens it and pours a whole lot of small tech devices onto the ground.* SAM *picks one up.*

SAM: This stuff could be anything.

MAX *grabs a device.*

MAX: This is a Twelve-G, ultra-slim, easy-to-hide tracking device. It has geofencing, which is a type of—

SAM: Virtual-boundary set-up. I know what it is.

MAX: Exactly. Like an invisible wall around your school or suburb.

TOBY: So that they know where you are at all times and if you go anywhere they don't want you to—

SAM: Where did you get these?

TOBY: Off the other kids who moved into the street.

SAM: Okay. I'm not sure what the deal is?

Beat.

Hang on. I get it! This is one of those Swayer pranks, right? You video me getting suckered, then it goes viral. Where are the cameras?

He waves his arms around.

Hey everyone! Funny! Real funny. Yep, you got me good! Woohoo? Come out, come out, wherever you are??

SAM *looks around the yard.* MIXIE *blocks his path. She stares at him seriously.*

You need to stop with the staring thing. It's freaking me out.

MIXIE: You're being tracked and monitored.

MAX: On the app. On every device you use, plus the street drones and cameras.

SAM: And? Your point?

TOBY: You and your mum—

SAM: How do you know it's just me and my mum?

MIXIE: We know quite a bit about you.

TOBY: You've been relocated.

>TOBY *looks at* MAX *and* MIXIE, *conflicted.*

SAM: [*sarcasm*] Ohhh. And here I was, thinking that we'd moved here because my mum got a new job in C-Zone.

TOBY: You were moved by the Regulators.

MIXIE: Can we fast-track things a little?

TOBY: Patience, Mixie.

MIXIE: He can only be seen going around the block for fifteen minutes more before they start to get suspicious.

TOBY: Sam, I know this might seem ... strange.

SAM: You think?

MIXIE: It's useless. He doesn't get it.

TOBY: You're being monitored—

SAM: Mum doesn't even use the tracker app anymore.

>*The trio look at each other.*

What?

TOBY: Your mum isn't the one tracing you.

SAM: Ahhhh. [*Dramatic*] The Regulators!!! Dum dum daaaaah!!

>MIXIE *pinching* SAM*'s arm.*

Owww.

MIXIE: Your moving here wasn't a mistake.

TOBY: This is not a street you just *move* into Sam! C-Zone is ... different.

>*Silence.*

SAM: Dudes! I don't want to disrespect your hood. But this is a pretty ordinary street. Trees, houses and some crappy lawn. Your skate park down the road is pretty cool, but apart from that it's an average, normal, typical—it's just / a street.

TOBY: You were moved here because ...

>*Pause.*

SAM: Yeah?

TOBY: It's complicated.

SAM: Try me.

MAX: It's about ... algorithms.

SAM: This keeps getting better and bet—

> MIXIE *elbowing* SAM *in the ribs. He is slightly winded.*

errrrhh. You hit me again and I will not hold back.

TOBY: Tell him Max.

MAX: [*formally*] Algorithms help us solve problems. We use computer language to—

SAM: Whitespace, Python, Intercal. Coding! I know what algorithms are, okay? What's this got to do with taking my phone?

MIXIE: Just listen.

> *Pause.*

MAX: Algorithms were once invisible, embedded in the background.

TOBY: No-one used to notice them. They were just circulating through the social world, making everything more efficient.

MAX: Until they started to sort and filter more and more things.

SAM: That's just progress and good programming.

TOBY: Except when all the decision-making is being done by 'something' else, telling us what we should purchase, how to dress and behave—

SAM: That's just persuasive advertising.

> MAX *uses a different tack.*

MAX: But what if our information searches were being censored and limited?

> *Beat.*

Tap in any subject, and it selects the top-five sites for you, right?

SAM: A page rank. So?

MAX: Click or search again. Same information. Keep clicking. It comes up with the same information again, only this time, under different titles, paragraphs shifted around a little to make it seem different.

TOBY: Algorithms are controlling what information we have access to.

SAM: Algorithms are man-made.

MIXIE: What if we told you that the programmers lost control?

SAM *remembering the computer breakdown and the fleeting images he saw in his bedroom.*

MAX: Algorithms are selecting the information it want us to see and hiding the rest.

SAM: Okay, and why would it do that?

MIXIE: [*mocking*] Let me see … To gain control of humankind.

SAM: That's ridiculous!

MIXIE: They're making every decision.

MAX: They're altering the facts to align everyone's way of thinking.

MIXIE: Think about it … Organisations, corporations, banks, the Government. They're all run by Algorithms.

MAX: Every institution is owned by them. Including schools.

Pause.

TOBY: But they need to control the risks.

Beat.

You were relocated to C-Zone, because you hacked Larry Page's code.

MAX: All of us were sent here because we crossed a line.

TOBY: Mixie's the one who exposed the fake image-enhancement used on Grenenger's beauty posts!

SAM: That was you?

MIXIE: Don't look so surprised.

TOBY: Max released a whole bunch of recordings from old radio stations and music that existed before the formula took over.

SAM: What formula?

MAX: All songs meet an algorithmic formula.

SAM: They do?

MAX: Years ago, there used to be lots of different music, bands and radio stations.

Pause.

TOBY: We need your help.

SAM: What with?

TOBY: Cracking a code.

SAM: What does the code do?

TOBY: We can't tell you that yet.

SAM: Then I can't help you. The code could be corrupt. I don't even know you and my plan is to keep out of trouble while I'm here.

Silence.

I think I should get going.

SAM *attempting to collect his board.* MIXIE *stands in his way.*

Just give me my phone and board.

MIXIE: Okay Max. Hit him with the facts.

MAX *takes out a device and reads aloud.*

MAX: Sam Turing. Behavioural concerns. I had to summarise this, coz your rap sheet is quite extensive. February fourth, late for classes three and seven. Yada, yada yada. February seventh, alternative opinions to teacher in charge. February twentieth, encouraging other students to challenge authority figures based on point of view varying from the model. March second, postings on social media … anti-Swayer comments. Policies on fashion, music and reading material have been breached. March fourth, regression report. Blah, blah, blaaah … March eighth, reading uncensored material, March tenth, postings not appropriate, March twenty-fifth, code hack. Serious violation. Relocation activated.

SAM: What the—how did you get that information?

MAX: School server systems are easy to hack.

TOBY: The point is, you've really annoyed the algorithm. You've been sent to C-Zone for—

Pause.

SAM: What?

MIXIE: Just tell him Toby.

TOBY: Alignment.

SAM: Right. So, you're telling me that I've been moved here because I 'accidentally' hacked a code? That's nuts. I'm a kid.

MIXIE: Rumour is … you had a book. Is that true?

TOBY: You've caused some major angst. Messages have been flying on the Whisper Net—

MAX: That's how we found out you were coming here.

TOBY: Is it true that you tripped the code? What did you see?

Pause. SAM *is unable to ignore the coincidences.*

SAM: I remember doing History homework and finding some information, that was different to the stuff I'd been taught.

MIXIE: From the book?

MAX: Where is it now? The book?

SAM: Vanished.

MIXIE: How?

SAM: I had a problem with my computer. I tried to override and go manual on the search and it was like it … It was …

    Pause.

MAX: Like what?

SAM: It's stupid.

TOBY: Try us.

SAM: Like the computer was purposely trying to stop me. I kept receiving notifications … and then—

    Silence. We hear crackling and whispering sounds. Flashback to the end of the opening scene.

FLASHBACK: THE TECHNICIANS

Sam's bedroom. SAM *hides the book. The chorus become the* CI *voices, Sam's* MUM, TECHNICIANS *and a* DELIVERY PERSON.

CI SIX: Dinnertime, Sam. Please make your way to the kitchen zone.

CI THREE: Study time ended. Power off.

    SAM *exits the room. A start-up sound.*

CI THREE: Violation of code four-seven-nine and three-zero-four.

CI FIVE: Contact Z team to retrieve illegal reading material.

SIGRID: Complete.

    The door signals a visitor.

SAM'S MUM: Can you get that, Sam?

    SAM *goes to the door and finds two* Z TECHNICIANS *waiting.*

TECH ONE: We have received an alert.

SAM: Alert for what?

TECH TWO: A system malfunction.

SAM: I didn't notify anyone.

TECH TWO: It's automatic.

TECH ONE: Direct from your system assistant.

SAM: Sigrid?

TECH TWO: Correct.

Pause.

May we enter?

SAM: We're just about to have dinner.

They enter.

TECH ONE: Please go ahead and have dinner. We won't be long.

SAM: I can show you where the main station is if you like?

TECH TWO: We know where it is.

Awkward silence.

Thank you for your assistance, young man.

SAM *attempts to follow the* TECHNICIANS *but the door signals again. It's a bouncy* DELIVERY PERSON *at the front doorstep, carrying a skateboard.*

DELIVERY: You must be Sam Turing! Congratulations! You've just won a replica vintage Tony Hawk Birdhouse. It comes with a hard rock maple deck, raw finish trucks, fifty-two-millimetre wheels for a softer ride.

SAM: I didn't enter the competition.

DELIVERY: [*checking screen* of *handheld device*] Sam Turing. That's you right?

SAM: Yeah but—

DELIVERY: You won it. Seriously cool, right?

Hands the board to SAM.

It comes completely assembled and ready to roll. With compliments from the Dillon Twins. Skate on, dude!

SAM *is confused. The* TECHNICIANS *walk out past* SAM *and the* DELIVERY PERSON.

SAM: Hey!

The TECHNICIANS *keep walking.*

DELIVERY: Alright. Gotta go now. Have fun!

    SAM *is left standing at the door. He watches them go.*

THE BACKYARD

Crackling. Whispers. A crow. We are in the backyard again.

SAM: When I went back to my bedroom—
TOBY: The book was gone.

    SAM *nods.*

MAX: They took it.
MIXIE: I've always wanted to see a book.
MAX: What was in it? It must have been pretty—I mean, here you are in C-Zone.
TOBY: They were scared that it would influence his opinions.
SAM: One kid's opinion is not going to change anything.
TOBY: Opinions are everything—
MAX: And too much variation can cause … Confusion.
MIXIE: Debate.
TOBY: Chaos.

    Beat.

That's why they created the Swayers. Like the Dillon Twins and Grenenger / and …
MIXIE: And the rest of them. Everyone is so busy trying to be like them—
SAM: Not me.
MAX: Whether you like it or not, they set the standard.
SAM: An impossible standard.
MAX: What about your mum?
SAM: What's she got to do with this?
MIXIE: She's been trying to keep you out of trouble.
TOBY: Cleaned up your profile page. Enhanced your images. That sort of thing.
SAM: She just likes to make a good impression. Everyone does it? Don't they?

    MAX *nods in agreement.*

MAX: She's doing it to protect you.

SAM: From?

> *Pause.*

MIXIE: Can you remember any people coming to your door? Serious people, wearing glasses like this.

> MIXIE *puts on some glasses.*

SAM: They used to come round to our house all the time. Technicians. We had problems with our receiver. We were in a dead spot or something.

> *Silence. Sombre mood.*

TOBY: Regulators only come around when there are … concerns.

> SAM *is silent. He's thinking. Flashback to Sam's old home.*

FLASHBACK: THE REGULATORS

Crackling and whispers. A door sound and we are back at Sam's old home.

MUM: [*calling*] Sam! Can you get that? Sam! Don't worry. I've got it.

> *Opening the door. There are two* REGULATORS *wearing identical glasses.*

[*Whispering*] What is it this time? I made all the changes to the images. I checked it against the guidelines.

REGULATOR TWO: There has been a lodgement regarding behavioural deviation.

MUM: Deviation. Again?

REGULATOR ONE: Reports that Sam is not aligning with social expectations.

MUM: I've checked everything. Clothing, profile—Sigrid is using a Friend Select App to try to get him to socialise a bit more. Are you sure this report is correct?

REGULATOR TWO: Are you implying that we have made an error, Mrs Turing?

MUM: [*correcting herself*] No. No, sorry. I hadn't noticed any—

REGULATOR ONE: Deviations?

The two REGULATORS *exchange glances.*

REGULATOR TWO: We exercised some tolerance after the loss of your husband …

MUM: Sam just needs some more time.

REGULATOR ONE: Mrs Turing, this is our fifth visit.

Silence.

Today you will be issued with a warning.

MUM: What does that mean?

REGULATOR ONE: Surely you want your son to be successful, happy and well adjusted?

MUM: Yes, of course—

REGULATOR TWO: School data indicates that his credit ranking is—

MUM: Low. Yes, but we're working on that. Sigrid / is monitoring—

REGULATOR ONE: We recommend that you work a little harder.

REGULATOR TWO: Keep a closer eye on your son, Mrs Turing.

A sinister crow is heard.

JUST NOD A LOT

We are in the backyard.

MIXIE: They were the Regulators!

SAM: [*uneasy*] This isn't funny anymore. I wanna go now.

MIXIE: You're in denial, Sam.

TOBY: It's normal. We all went through it too.

Pause.

SAM: What happens to the kids who …

TOBY: Don't align?

Pause.

MAX: They change.

SAM: I'm not changing anything.

TOBY: You don't get a choice.

MAX *looks nervously over the fence.*

MAX: We don't have long.

MIXIE: I'd say three minutes max.

SAM: I've been skating round the block, right?

TOBY: They'll be checking that now. The cameras will show that you haven't been to the skate park, so if anyone asks, tell them that you found an urban ramp between Curtis and Sky Street.

SAM: Won't they have cameras there?

TOBY: It's a weak spot. Unreliable cameras.

SAM: How will I know who the Swayers are?

MIXIE: You'll work it out.

MAX: Be careful who you trust. They've used your screen-gnome so they know exactly what you like to talk about, your interests, purchases … everything. They'll be pairing you up with some … friends.

TOBY: About that … Sam, you gotta try make some friends, so that they don't suspect anything.

SAM: I don't have a great track record in that area.

MIXIE: Just agree with everything they say.

TOBY: Start wearing the same things. Change your style to match.

SAM: Why?

TOBY: They'll think you're getting better, you know, aligning.

SAM: Why have you told me all of this?

MAX: We need your help.

TOBY: I haven't told you everything yet. But enough to get you through the next couple of days. There's stuff going on in C-Zone. Bad stuff.

MAX *retrieves* SAM*'s phone for him.* MIXIE *returns his skateboard.*

I'll be in your history class. Better pretend you don't know me. I'll explain later.

Beat.

Don't get Watcher angry.

SAM: Who's that?

MIXIE: Educational Guidance AI.

TOBY: Don't post anything that might affect your rankings.

MAX: Don't ask too many questions. Just nod a lot.

MAX *demonstrates.*

MIXIE: Try not to stand out.

TOBY: Make sure your schoolwork is … what they ask for.

MIXIE: Don't be too clever. [*Joking*] Shouldn't be too hard?

MAX: Or inventive. Just nod a lot.

TOBY: We'll be in contact.

WATCHER'S WARNING

The next morning, at C-Zone High. SAM *is in the middle of history class.* TOBY *is present. The class are wearing virtual reality goggles. Sounds of conflict, sad music and an educational voiceover are played. The class can be mobile, moving around and scattered. There are no formal desks and chairs in this classroom. A* VOICEOVER *booms.* STUDENTS *respond in shock and surprise.*

VIDEO: [*voiceover*] Prior to our current System of Government, organised by Algorithms, our world was in chaos. World conflicts were brutal. Catastrophic. Corruption was commonplace and unemployment at an all-time high. Now see Conflict Forty-two. Pre-Algorithmic organisation and stability, people lived in fear—

WATCHER: And that concludes our lesson. We can all count ourselves very lucky to be living without conflict, poverty and unemployment. All thanks to the System and our wonderful Regulators.

All STUDENTS *clap except* SAM. *They turn simultaneously and stare at him.* TOBY *silently urges him to clap.* SAM *claps and the class turns back to* WATCHER.

You are now dismissed for a short break. Please use the time wisely.

The class depart.

Sam Turing, would you please stay behind?

SAM *is still.* WATCHER *slowly advances. The effect is menacing.*

Welcome to C-Zone Secondary. We are very excited to have you join us. I've heard that you're a very bright student with great potential. Unfortunately, your records also indicate a tendency to … agitate. I'm sure that this is just a phase. But Sam, please understand that we do things a little differently at C-Zone. Any deviations can and will result in punishment. Do we understand each other?

SAM: Yes.

WATCHER: I will be watching.

WATCHER *stares at* SAM *then departs.*

THE SWAYERS

SAM *attempts to exit and is stopped by three perfect-looking friends. Awkward silence.*

JAKE: Hey Sam, I'm Jake, this is Luca and Tay. You want a tour?

SAM: Thanks, but I've already had a look around and I've got to go pick up my course files.

TAY: I hear you skate?

SAM: How did you know that?

TAY: You came up on my feed. You've got some cool moves.

JAKE: Yeah, can you show me how you do that backside tail kick?

SAM: Ummm, yeah. No problems.

JAKE: You met any other crew from school yet?

> SAM *shakes his head.* TAY, JAKE *and* LUCA *exchange glances.*

TAY: One thing you need to know, Sam. There are some truly strange cats at this school. When I first arrived, that girl, Mixie and her friends tried to convince me that there was some massive conspiracy going on. Mixie stands for mixed up.

LUCA: Totally gone.

JAKE: [*to* LUCA] Unkind, dude. [*To* SAM] Let's rephrase that. They're imaginative kids, but you don't want to get mixed up with them.

SAM: Why not?

JAKE: They're nuts.

LUCA: And what about your rankings?

TAY: Remember Alex? She hung out with them and it was social suicide. Rankings took a serious dive.

> *He makes a bomb whistle and explosion sound.*

LUCA: What happened to Alex?

TAY: Just dropped off the radar.

SAM: Anyway … I don't know them.

> LUCA *stares at* SAM *suspiciously.*

LUCA: It's a cool skateboard you got there Sam. Looks exactly like the one in the Dillon Twins competition.

As they speak the following dialogue, they surround SAM. *It should sound like a threatening commercial.*

JAKE: The retro, Tony Hawk, Birdhouse.

TAY: Seven-ply maple deck, laser logo trucks. Cool!

Awkward silence.

JAKE: So, we'll meet you at the skate park after school?

SAM: Gotta help my mum unpack.

TAY: Easy. We'll swing by your place and pick you up tomorrow.

SAM: Sorry, busy tomorrow too.

JAKE: Weekend it is then.

SAM *watches them leave. He shudders.*

SAM IN THE SILENCER

TOBY *quietly approaches* SAM, *tapping him on the shoulder.*

SAM: Geez! Scared the—

TOBY *indicates to cameras and beckons* SAM *to follow. They step into a hallway and* TOBY *indicates that this is a dead spot for cameras, takes out a small device and places it at their feet. They turn it on and it emits an orange light around them.*

SAM: What is it?

TOBY: A plasmapheric silencer. It means we can talk without anyone seeing or hearing us.

SAM: I read about these.

TOBY: What did Watcher want?

SAM: Nothing.

TOBY: How about Jake and the others?

SAM: They asked me to go skating.

TOBY: That's it?

TOBY *suddenly stops, indicates for* SAM *to remain quiet. We hear a buzzing sound.* WATCHER *and a group of* REGULATORS *walk past* SAM *and* TOBY. WATCHER *stops suddenly, halting the others, listens carefully and moves so close to* SAM *that his eyes almost pop out of his head.* TOBY *and* SAM *hold their breath.*

WATCHER *decides it was nothing and beckons to the others to move on.*

A little too close.

SAM: Creepy.

TOBY: Watcher's got advanced built-in sensors. Probably picked up on some slight movement or breathing.

SAM: I wouldn't want to get on their wrong side.

Pause.

TOBY: I've got a detention with them soon.

SAM: What for?

TOBY: It's a regular thing.

Beat.

Can you meet us / this afternoon—

SAM: I've got stuff I need to do.

TOBY *looks desperately at* SAM.

TOBY: We really need you—

SAM: Sorry. We're still unpacking and I've got an assignment to finish / and—

TOBY *realising that* SAM *is making excuses.*

TOBY: Just say it, Sam. You think we're a bit weird … or is it to do with our social ranking—which one is it?

SAM: Neither. I'm new and I don't want to get into any trouble.

TOBY: I hate to break it to you, Sam, but you're in trouble, right now … and you're going to need some friends whether you like it or not.

Pause.

Let's hope you choose the right ones. Gotta go.

TOBY *collecting the plasmapheric silencer, puts on their glasses and suddenly the hallways are alive with* STUDENTS *travelling to and from classes.* SAM *puts his glasses on and he sees directions to his next class.*

PIGGY

Afternoon. The hallways are empty until we hear crackling and whispers and then the following taunts are delivered.

VOICES: Here piggy wiggy. Chubby, fatty. Fatso. Wobble boy.

MAX *scuttling down the hallway as fast as he can looking back over his shoulder, panicked. He is being pursued by a group of* STUDENTS.

STUDENT ONE: Hey fatso!

STUDENT TWO: You're gonna give yourself a heart attack.

STUDENT THREE: Slow down, marshmallow boy.

MAX *runs, crashing straight into another group, surrounded.*

STUDENT FOUR: Get him!

The STUDENTS *grab him.* STUDENT FIVE *brings out a set of scales.*

STUDENT FIVE: Okay fatty. Time for your weekly weigh-in.

STUDENT ONE: Get on the scales.

MAX: No.

STUDENT FIVE: Did you hear that?

STUDENTS *all reply with yep, nods and other responses. They hold* MAX *tighter.*

MAX: You're hurting me.

STUDENT FIVE: Awwwww! Poor piggy wiggy.

STUDENTS *laugh.* STUDENT FIVE *walking menacingly closer to* MAX.

Get—on—the scales.

Frightened, MAX *gets on the scales. They all look at the weight and make noises of disappointment.*

Doesn't look like you've made any progress, pig.

MAX: Everyone's built differently.

STUDENT FOUR: Do you see anyone here who looks like you?

MAX: I'm not fat.

STUDENT TWO: The scales say that you are.

STUDENT FIVE *twists* MAX*'s ear. He is close to tears.*

STUDENT FIVE: Look at yourself. The way you dress, walk, talk. No-one likes looking at you when you come into class anymore. Your credit rankings are low. It's affecting the whole school. You're letting everyone down.

STUDENT FIVE *moves closer to* MAX.

I don't care how smart you are, stupid! Get your credits up. Understand?

The others bend his arm high up his back. MAX *reels in pain.*

MAX: Yeeesss.

STUDENT FIVE: You've got two weeks to improve your look, buy some decent brands, smarten up … and if you don't …

They release him and he falls hard. A beeping sound signals the end of the school day. The STUDENTS *leave, taunting him as they go. The hallways start to fill.* SAM *sees* MAX *getting up from the ground. They lock eyes.* MAX *wipes his eyes and leaves.* SAM *watches him walk away.*

MIXED-UP MIXIE

The next day SAM *is on his skateboard heading to school.* JAKE, LUCA *and* TAY *appear.* SAM *stalls to a halt.*

JAKE: Hey.
SAM: Hey.
LUCA: Hey.
TAY: Hey.

Silence.

JAKE: You getting the hang of things round here yet?
SAM: Not sure.
LUCA: Nothing to it, Sammy.
TAY: It's all easy in the C.
JAKE: You just need a little bit of help.
SAM: What with?

JAKE: Your profile … It's a little …

TAY: Tired.

LUCA: We can help you with the status thing.

JAKE: You just need to get linked in with some big fish. Starting with us.

SAM: [*cautiously*] Right.

JAKE: You just need to establish some cred. Some cool posts, the right branding and some good connections.

SAM: Thanks, I'll think about it.

> MIXIE *enters. She is on her way to school. She tries to change direction but* JAKE *notices her and alerts the rest of the group.*

JAKE: Ahhh Wooo! Mixed-up Mixie.

LUCA: You know Mixie, don't you Sam? Mixie knows all about taking a serious nosedive on the social scene.

JAKE: Did you know that she has a black belt?

> JAKE, LUCA *and* TAY *striking martial arts poses that are exaggerated and meant to ridicule.*

MIXIE: Shut up, Jake.

JAKE: Come on Mix. Is that any way to behave in front of our new friend?

> JAKE *circles* MIXIE.

Mixie tells some fantastic stories.

LUCA: Unbelievable.

MIXIE: [*to* SAM] Enjoying the company?

TAY: Mixed-up Mixie, alright.

> MIXIE *walks up to* TAY.

MIXIE: Tay. If you were twice as smart—

TAY: Yeah?

MIXIE: You'd still be stupid.

> TAY *launches forward but* MIXIE *is too quick.*

JAKE: Hey Sam, if you need to get any additional advice on how to completely ruin your reputation. I bet Mixie would be happy to help out.

> TAY *laughs for a little too long.* MIXIE *walks toward* TAY.

MIXIE: Shh. Did you hear that?

TAY: What?

MIXIE: It's the sound of no-one caring.

> TAY *tries to launch at her again.* MIXIE *is too quick.* SAM *is secretly impressed.*

LUCA: Ahhh wooooo!

> MIXIE *gives them a resolute finger and attempts to walk on.* JAKE *stops her.*

JAKE: [*whispering*] That's going to hurt later on, Mix.

> *He looks at* SAM *and fakes a heartbreak, holding hand on heart. They all laugh.* MIXIE *looks at* SAM *and departs.*

Skate park, Saturday. Around ten.

> *He approaches* SAM.

Don't stand us up.

> *They exit in the same direction as* MIXIE.

TOBY'S FIGHT

In the detention room again. TOBY *is in a chair with earphones on. The earphones flash and buzz with light and each flash causes discomfort for* TOBY. *We hear what they hear. Advertisements, with awful jingles, Swayers talking about the latest trends and crazes, all played at a deafening volume. It is relentless.* TOBY *sits looking slightly tired but defiant.* WATCHER *circles once and signals to the* REGULATOR *in control of the program.*

WATCHER: Stop! Stop. [*To the* REGULATOR] Unfortunately, we cannot go to full alteration mode until I get the information I need.

> *She wipes some hair from* TOBY*'s face, gently.*

One flick of a switch and this could all be over. Quick and painless. You won't remember a thing. But if you continue to be stubborn and obstinate—if you refuse to give us what we know you have … this will be drawn out. Excruciating. Unbearable. All you have to do / is give us—

TOBY: I haven't taken anything.

WATCHER: The code! We know you have it.

TOBY: What code?

WATCHER: The one designed by Hamilton. Such a talented coder. What a shame, she didn't fully appreciate the alterations we made to her program.

TOBY: What have you done with her?

WATCHER: She just vanished one day ... disappeared. Most unprofessional!

Beat.

We know she left you with the code. Now give it to me.

TOBY: If anyone finds out what you're doing here—

WATCHER: Stupid child! They already know. C-Zone is the approved centre for testing and everyone here has been ... selected to assist us with our experiment.

TOBY: You won't get away with this.

WATCHER: Really? Just watch us.

> WATCHER *signals to the* REGULATOR *to inflict another round of torture.* TOBY *stiffens.* WATCHER *signals again to halt the treatment.*

The code! Tell me where it is.

TOBY: I don't have it.

WATCHER: Lies! [*To the* REGULATOR] Again!!!

> *She signals to one of the* REGULATORS *to switch a button. We see the earphones flash and buzz as* TOBY *reels in pain.*

STICK TO THE PLAN

MIXIE is hiding in a cupboard. Suddenly the door opens. MIXIE *inhales sharply. It's* MAX. MIXIE *pulls him into the cupboard and shuts the door.*

MIXIE: What took you so long?

MAX: I was at the gym.

MIXIE: The gym? What were you—doesn't matter. Where's Toby?

MAX: Detention.

MIXIE: Again?

MAX: It will be one of us next time.

> MAX *sees bruises on her arm. He takes her arm gently and examines the bruise.*

Where did you get this?

MIXIE: Bumped into a pole.

MAX: A pole with fingers?

> *Silence.*

I'm gonna kill 'em.

MIXIE: Thanks, Max. But you wouldn't hurt a fly.

MAX: I would if it annoyed me enough.

MIXIE: You saved a cricket from an ant attack the other day.

MAX: Unfair odds for the cricket.

MIXIE: True.

MAX: It was Jake, Tay and the other idiot, right?

MIXIE: I can take care of myself.

> *Beat.*

You talk to Toby about a plan?

MAX: Sort of. You speak to Sam.

MIXIE: Waste of time.

MAX: Toby said / he's important—

MIXIE: Sam is a lost cause.

> *Beat.*

We've got part of the code. We just need to work out how to get the rest.

MAX: It's useless.

MIXIE: We just need more time.

MAX: We've been trying for months.

> *Pause.*

I can't do it. I can't crack it.

MIXIE: Hamilton had faith in you, Max.

MAX: Mistake number one.

MIXIE: She knew you'd find the code in the sheet music. We need to figure out the rest, revisit everything she taught us.

MAX: It's too hard and we don't even know if it'll work.

MIXIE: It has to.

MAX: I'm not good enough.

MIXIE: You're the smartest guy I know.

MAX: Stop saying that … You'll only be disappointed.

>*Pause.*

And I'm sick of disappointing people.

MIXIE: You listen to me, Max Goodart. The other part of the code is out there somewhere. While I finish the search, you keep trying to crack the code.

MAX: You don't even know what you're looking for.

>*Pause.*

Watcher has started work on Toby. I've already noticed … changes.

>*Silence.*

MIXIE: That means we've only got a matter of days.

>MIXIE *looks at* MAX, *pleading.*

MAX: I'll keep trying.

>MIXIE *hugs* MAX. *She opens the cupboard door tentatively. Then exits. Heading down the hallway,* MIXIE *collides with a bunch of* GIRLS. *They are perfectly coordinated.*

GRENENGER: There she is! Mixie!

>MIXIE *ignores the girl.*

Why do you have to be so rude?

>MIXIE *goes to leave.*

We have a message from Toby.

>MIXIE *stops.*

MIXIE: What is it?

GRENENGER: If you use a friendlier tone, I might give you the message.

>MIXIE *turning to leave.*

Shame. Toby really needs to see you too.

>MIXIE *turns back and approaches* GRENENGER.

MIXIE: Tell me what it is, or I'll rearrange your look.

GRENENGER: I'll tell you where Toby is if you subscribe to my page.

MIXIE: I predict that you will tell me where she is in ten seconds.

> GRENENGER *laughs.* MIXIE *grabs* GRENENGER *in a hand-lock and has her reeling in pain.* GIRL TWO *steps forward to defuse the heated situation.*

GIRL TWO: It's the truth. Toby is looking for you.

> MIXIE *twisting* GRENENGER *'s hand.*

GIRL ONE: She wasn't feeling well.

GIRL TWO: We tried to help her, but she asked for you.

GIRL THREE: She was throwing up and everything.

GIRL FOUR: It wasn't pretty.

> *Pause.*

MIXIE: Where is she?

GIRL ONE *and* TWO: Biology room.

GIRL THREE: The storage room at the back.

> MIXIE *releases* GRENENGER *'s hand and shoves her back toward the* GIRLS.

GRENENGER: Watcher will hear about this.

> MIXIE *exits hurriedly. The* GIRLS *help* GRENENGER *up.*

I hope she gets exactly what she deserves …

> *Menacing whispers are heard.*

TOBY'S CHANGE

In a hallway at school. SAM *spots* TOBY *and catches up with them.* TOBY *has changed and needs to sound overly positive, like a sales pitch.*

SAM: Hey Toby.

TOBY: [*saccharine*] Hi Sam. [*Looking him up and down*] Tick! Tick! You're looking dapper today.

SAM: Are you okay?

TOBY: Great. Like summer. Is that a new Singe shirt your wearing?

SAM: I don't know.

TOBY: It's singin'!

SAM: What language are you speaking?

TOBY: See you in History. Later.

> *Pause.* TOBY *shakes her head in frustration. A moment of clarity.* TOBY *rushes to* SAM.

Sam. Sam. Time … it's running away … you have to help Max—

> TOBY *shakes her head again. Clicks into the advertisement voice again.*

Later!

SAM: What?

> WATCHER *has entered the hallway and has moved silently to stand beside* SAM.

WATCHER: You look perplexed, Sam?

> SAM *is shocked that they snuck up on him so stealthily.*

It's time for our validation meeting.

> SAM *looks confused.*

The whole school assembles in the hall for any announcements. Hurry along.

> WATCHER *indicates to the glasses in his hand.* SAM *puts on his glasses and exits.*

VALIDATION MEETING

We are now in the hall with the entire school. The assembly is underway. A STUDENT *is mid-speech.*

STUDENT THREE: Chiara has exceeded two thousand two hundred hits for her gorgeous beach shots. What made her upload so unique, was the super-clever use of angles which highlighted her look. Oh, and for all you girls out there … the bikinis were all from Singe, Celeb and Focus. Get shopping and well done, Chiara!!

> *Applause.*

STUDENT TWO: This award goes to my man, Nash, for skyrocketing to number two in popularity for his comedy video and crazy bottle-flipping stunt. Dude, you must have spent days trying to get that shot. But it's paid off. Nice work.

Applause.

WATCHER: I am pleased to announce that C-Zone now has over sixteen million subscribers which moves us into a highly satisfactory range.

Applause.

Unfortunately, there are individuals amongst us who, despite our best efforts … continue to negatively affect our school brand. I am sorry to report that one student from C-Zone has slipped to an unacceptable level. His laziness is holding us back from achieving our ultimate goal. Max Goodart, please come up to the stage.

MAX *looks around, embarrassed. He is then pushed up to* WATCHER.

The algorithm predicted that Max would add unnecessary stress to our healthcare system later in life. This was proven after analysis of his personal data. The recommendation was that he attend the gymnasium four times a week, but our records show that he only attended twice. Other data reveals that he exceeded the recommended calorie intake for someone of his … build. His choices show a complete disregard for our public profile. Therefore, to assist him to get back on the right path, I will be releasing an image of Max. Hopefully, this will remind him to set goals and stick to them. Would everyone put on their glasses and wait for the upload.

Everyone puts glasses on. A beeping sounds emits throughout the crowd of STUDENTS *as they receive an image of* MAX. *There are gasps, groans and laughter.*

Put on your glasses, Max.

MAX *slowly puts on his glasses. A beep. The assembly erupts with laughter. We see* MAX's *body stiffen then slump. He is mortified, humiliated and miserable. He runs out of the hall. The laughter dies down.*

That will be all. Dismissed.

The STUDENTS *leave.* SAM *follows* MAX.

MIXIE TRICKED

MIXIE *is on her way to the biology room to meet* TOBY. *The room is dark.*

MIXIE: Toby? Toby? It's Mixie. You okay?

She walks on until she is inside the biology room. There are specimens in jars all around her. Suddenly the door closes. JAKE, TAY *and* LUCA *surround her.*

JAKE: Mixie, Mixie, Mixie. We need to have a little chat.

LUCA: A talk.

TAY: It won't take long.

MIXIE: I'm guessing Toby's not here.

JAKE: Toby? She'll be back soon.

MIXIE: Liar!

TAY: She was feeling sick so …

LUCA: They went to the bathroom.

They approach MIXIE, *attempting to drive her into a corner.*

JAKE: That's right.

MIXIE: I'm late for class.

Beat.

JAKE: You made us look stupid in front of our new friend.

LUCA: That's right.

MIXIE: No, I didn't.

TAY: Huh?

MIXIE: You did that all by yourselves.

LUCA: What?

JAKE: You're gonna pay, Mixie!

They launch at MIXIE. *She dodges them. The three of them are now cornered.* MIXIE *quickly grabs a jar off the shelf, takes a big breath and holds it. She unscrews the lid. The smell of formaldehyde fills the room. The boys cough and gag.* MIXIE *runs.*

GET HER!

MIXIE *sprints out the door. They follow, coughing and spluttering as they go. She dodges and weaves through groups of* STUDENTS *down the hallways. This slows her down. She makes her way outside, but the* BOYS *are gaining.* SAM *sees* MIXIE *running. He indicates to a hiding spot.* MIXIE *takes cover. The* BOYS *stop, perplexed.* SAM *stares at* MIXIE *willing her to stay quiet.*

LUCA: She went this way.

JAKE: You sure?

TAY: She's headed toward Toby's place. It's this way.

JAKE: Split up. [*To* LUCA] You go that way. [*To* TAY] Head to Toby's. I'll roll past Max's. Meet you at the skate park in ten.

> *They take off in different directions.* SAM *signs for* MIXIE *to stay where she is.* SAM *comes out from and just as he does* LUCA *returns.*

LUCA: What's up Sammy?

SAM: Heading home. You?

LUCA: You see anyone come past here?

SAM: Just that kid who wears the green hat. Tall. You know the one?

LUCA: Outland or the Singe hat?

SAM: What's the difference?

LUCA: The Outland has the circle symbol on the left-hand side and the Singe has an 'S' on the brim.

SAM: Singe.

LUCA: Yep. Cool hat. Gotta go.

> LUCA *exits.* SAM *breathes a sigh of relief. He signals to* MIXIE *that the coast is clear.*

SAM: You okay?

MIXIE: [*clearly upset*] Yes!

> *Pause.* MIXIE *wells up with tears. She starts to pace, breathing heavily.*

No.

SAM: Stop and breathe.

> MIXIE *speaks hurriedly, it all comes out in a jumble as if she is in shock.*

MIXIE: There's no time, Sam. We're in serious trouble … Now! I've been looking everywhere to find something. But we don't understand the clue. I don't know where Toby is. If we don't find the rest of the code, I'll end up starting my own makeup range and talking like a Swayer—Max doesn't think he can finish it and—

SAM: Whoa! Finish what?

MIXIE: The code. It's designed to corrupt the program—

SAM: What program?

MIXIE: The program that's making everyone sound …

SAM: Like a walking TV commercial?

MIXIE *nods.*

Tell me about the program.

MIXIE: It was designed by Hamilton. An amazing coding teacher from C-Zone … before everything went bad. The algorithm hijacked their work and now Watcher is using the program to alter the human mind.

SAM: [*to himself*] They're aligning everyone.

MIXIE: What?

SAM: I saw Toby today. She was …

MIXIE *slumps in resignation.*

MIXIE: It won't be long before we're next.

SAM: You said the code will corrupt the program. How do you know?

MIXIE: Hamilton left a message for us in some sheet music with a clue. Max is the only one who plays. They must have known he would find it. Except we can't figure it out.

SAM: A musical cryptogram.

Beat.

Did this Hamilton leave any clues about where to find the other part of the code?

MIXIE: Three words, 'it—is—here'. Except that it's not. I've looked everywhere.

SAM: Can I take a look at the sheet music?

MIXIE: Max has it.

Beat.

SAM: Is he okay?

MIXIE: Who? Max?

SAM: What Watcher did to him today was wrong …

MIXIE: What are you talking about?

SAM: The validation meeting.

MIXIE: What happened?

SAM: Put your glasses on.

> MIXIE *puts her glasses on, a beep signals and the image of* MAX *in his underwear downloads.* MIXIE *looks shocked, then angry. She slowly, removes the glasses.*

MIXIE: Poor Max.

> *Beat.*

We need to get to the backyard now.

SAM: What happened to this teacher, the coder, Hamilton?

MIXIE: Disappeared.

SAM: Not helpful—

MIXIE: Hamilton was being monitored. That's why he broke the code up. Watcher and the Regulators have been tearing the place apart looking for it too. It's a race to see who gets there first.

SAM: Let's find Max.

> SAM *starts to leave and* MIXIE *stops him.*

MIXIE: We need to dodge the cameras. This way.

> MIXIE *and* SAM *leave.*

MAX

MAX *is sitting up on a lookout platform in the backyard. He is staring into nothing.* SAM *and* MIXIE *arrive.*

MIXIE: Max!

> *Silence.*

Maxy?

> *Silence.*

You, okay?

> *No answer.*

MIXIE: [*forcefully*] Max! You come down here now or I'm gonna come / up there and—

MAX: Did you see it?

> *Pause.*

MIXIE: What? You in your swimwear?

> MAX *slumps and turns away.*

Like, I've never seen you in your swimmers before?

MAX: Underwear.

MIXIE: Swimmers, underwear. Who cares.

MAX: Everyone saw.

MIXIE: So?

MAX: They laughed.

MIXIE: They're idiots.

> *Beat.*

When have you ever cared what everyone thinks?

MAX: I don't.

MIXIE: Then get down here now.

MAX: Do you think I'm fat?

MIXIE: I think you're one of the smartest, caring, sweetest guys I know.

MAX: That wasn't the question.

> *Pause.*

MIXIE: You're not skinny …

> SAM *shoves* MIXIE. *She glares at him.*

SAM: [*whispering*] Real sensitive, Mixie.

MIXIE: [*whispering*] I'm being honest. Max is too smart for lies.

MAX: I'm fat.

MIXIE: Nope. No. That's not what I said.

MAX: They took a photo of me bending over. I looked like a baby hippo.

MIXIE: Yeah, so? Hippos are fierce, smart and protective.

MAX: There were big rolls hanging over my swimmers.

MIXIE: Alert! Max! Everyone has rolls. Especially when they bend over and if they haven't, then they're too skinny.

MAX: I'm disgusting.

> MIXIE *starts to climb the ladder.*

What are you doing?

MIXIE: What does it look like?

MAX: You hate heights.

> *She continues to climb.*

You'll freak out and freeze, like you did last time.

> *She continues to climb.*

And I'll have to coax you down and it'll take hours.

> *She continues to climb.*

Stop it!

> MIXIE *continues to climb, and* SAM *follows. They sit either side of* MAX. *Long silence.*

They all laughed. The whole school.

MIXIE: Did you laugh, Sam?

SAM: No. It wasn't funny.

MIXIE: See. They didn't *all* laugh.

MAX: [*sarcasm*] One person didn't laugh.

> *Silence.*

Still hurts.

> MIXIE *moves closer and puts her arm around* MAX.

That's a little too tight.

MIXIE: Yeah, I'm a bit petrified.

MAX: You're such a loon, Mix.

MIXIE: Just the way you like me, right?

> *Pause.*

MAX: Yeah.

MIXIE: And I like you the way you are.

> *Beat.*

Max?

MAX: Yeah?

MIXIE: You're a good-looking guy. But better than that, you're funny and smart and once they all find out how brilliant you are, then watch out! You'll have every girl lining up for a chance to hang out with you.

MAX: Girls?

MIXIE: Or boys? Or no-one?

They all sit in silence. SAM *has pangs of longing as he watches the two good friends.*

MAX: I'm going to need help … with the code.

They look at SAM.

SAM: I'm in.

MIXIE: Great.

Beat.

Now who's going to help me get down from here?

SAM *and* MAX *help* MIXIE *down and they huddle together discussing a plan.* MIXIE *leaves,* SAM *and* MAX *sit down to solve some coding problems.*

IT IS HEAR

The following montage of action/images needs to occur in quick succession with music underscoring to enhance the tension.

Image One

STUDENTS *walk across the stage. The movement is quite naturalistic. Until suddenly they all stop simultaneously, and in slow motion face toward the audience. The mood is sinister.*

Image Two

In the detention room. WATCHER *and the* REGULATORS *are seen having a meeting.* WATCHER *is issuing instructions.*

Image Three

JAKE *runs in, whistles to* LUCA *and* TAY *who enter.* JAKE *indicates that they are to split and meet back later. They are searching for* MIXIE. *They run offstage.*

Image Four

TOBY *appears, shaking their head.* TOBY *is fighting an internal battle against the personality-altering treatment.*

Image Five

SAM *and* MAX *are holding the sheet music. They are deep in problem-solving mode.*

Image Six

We see MIXIE *searching the school for the code. She hears a noise and moves quickly, with agility, to a hiding spot.* LUCA *passes her. She breathes a sigh of relief and then sprints off.*

Image Seven

Groups of STUDENTS *walk a militant and menacing sequence across the stage.*

Image Eight

SAM *and* MAX *look frustrated and resigned to failure.*

Image Nine

The REGULATORS *and* WATCHER *walk with urgency searching for evidence of the code.*

Image Ten

MIXIE *hides again. She stops suddenly. She looks at a light that is shining on the ground. She puts her hand under the light and examines it. She slowly looks up and we see an idea forming. She sprints off toward the backyard.* TOBY *appears and follows her.*

STEGANOGRAPHY

MAX *and* SAM *are in the backyard. They are exhausted and ready to give up.* MIXIE *arrives, puffing and unable to speak.*

MAX: Did you find it?

She waves her arms about trying to catch her breath.

SAM: Mixie?

MIXIE *shakes her head. Still unable to speak.*

MAX: That's it then. We're finished.

MAX *and* SAM *look dejected.* MIXIE *starts unpacking different-coloured plastics from her bag and a torch. She spreads the sheet music out and shines different colours onto it.*

What are you doing?

SAM *observes* MIXIE *and then slowly gets more involved. He is now handing different colours to her.*

SAM: Steganography? Mixie thinks Hamilton was using steganography.

MAX: Stega—what?

SAM: A concealed message within a message. She thinks the rest of the code is hidden on the sheet music itself. Old-school!

MAX: You mean like invisible ink?

MIXIE *tries the last colour. Nothing.* MAX *appears defeated.* SAM *is deep in thought.*

MIXIE: Sorry. I thought—

She indicates to the sheet music.

Hamilton said, 'it is here'. So, I thought ... Doesn't matter. We're finished.

MIXIE *is clearly upset. She walks away.* MAX *is looking carefully at the sheet music.*

MAX: Except she couldn't spell very well. She spelt it H-E-A-R instead of—

SAM *looks at* MAX *then looks at the sheet music and suddenly runs and collects the digital keyboard and puts it in front of* MAX.

SAM: Max, play the notes.

MAX: What?

SAM: Go. Now!

> MAX *plays.* SAM *records it with a device. He opens up the sound file on a spectrum analyser.*

Hamilton wants us to 'hear' H-E-A-R the music. What if the code is concealed in the sound itself?

Indicates to the device screen.

MIXIE: What is it?

MAX: It's a spectrogram.

SAM: We just need to insert the sound file ... and it should give us a visual representation of the sound waves. Like this ... and go!

> SAM *presses a button.* MIXIE *and* MAX *crowd around* SAM. *The music plays and a code appears.* MAX *starts noting it down furiously.*

MAX: That's it! You've done it Sam.

SAM: You did all the groundwork!

> MIXIE *hugs* SAM. *A moment.* MAX *high-fives* SAM.

MIXIE: What are you waiting for? Let's get to the school now.

> *They go to leave and* TOBY *blocks the way.*

TOBY: Don't move, Max!

> MIXIE *walks quickly over to* TOBY.

MIXIE: Toby?

TOBY: I'm warning you.

MIXIE: What are you talking about?

TOBY: Hand it over now.

MIXIE: [*to* MAX] Run.

TOBY: It's too late.

> *We hear the sound of drones and a menacing whisper. The* STUDENTS *approach in a zombie-like fashion.*

You've been tracked ... They're coming.

> MIXIE *grabs* TOBY *and, in one swift move, takes her legs out from under her, pinning her to the ground.*

MIXIE: Go Max! Now!!!!

> TOBY *struggles with* MIXIE. *We see the zombie-like* STUDENTS *approaching and the menacing whisper intensifies.*

SAM: Max! We've got to go.

MAX: I'm not leaving Mixie here.

> MIXIE *gains the upper hand and has* TOBY *pinned.*

MIXIE: If you don't move it now Max, I'm going to throw out all of your gadgets and then I'm going to sing that song you hate over and over and over again—

SAM: You know she'll do it. Come on!

MIXIE: I'll be fine. GO!!!

> MAX *reluctantly joins* SAM *and they run. The zombie* STUDENTS *reach* MIXIE. MIXIE *tries to defend herself but is completely overpowered. She disappears from view.*

THE SHOWDOWN

SAM *and* MAX *weave in and out of corridors making their way to* WATCHER*'s detention room. They hear a noise and* SAM *drags* MAX *into the shadows.* WATCHER *and the* REGULATORS *appear.*

WATCHER: Lock all gates and doors. Launch additional drones. We need to find those kids. If they have the code—all of our time, testing—everything we've achieved so far—will mean nothing. Tear the place apart if you have to … FIND THEM!!

> WATCHER *and the* REGULATORS *disperse and exit.* SAM *and* MAX *sneak down corridor and enter the detention room.*

SAM: That's it. That's the mainframe.

> MAX *walks toward the computer and, as he does, the whispering, crackling sound erupts.* MAX *suddenly freezes and cannot move.*

Max? Are you okay? Max!

> *The sound intensifies and* MAX *is frozen like a statue.*

MAX: I can't move.

SAM: You must be in a paralysis zone. Part of the security set-up. Hold on!

SAM *takes some small lights from his backpack and places them in a pattern around the mainframe.*

MAX: Hurry, Sam. I've tripped the alarm. They'll be here any second.

We hear sounds of a security pad being pressed.

SAM: When I say go. Run, Max.

SAM *places the last light and we hear a zapping sound and see a flash of light.* MAX *runs and starts inserting the code.* SAM *moves the lights to create a barrier between* MAX *and the* REGULATORS. *As they enter,* SAM *hides so that all they see is* MAX.

REGULATOR ONE: Stop right there!

REGULATOR TWO *runs toward* MAX *and gets stuck in the paralysis zone.* REGULATOR ONE *draws a weapon and aims it at* MAX.

SAM: Over here! Useless bag of bolts.

REGULATOR ONE *aims the weapon at* SAM *who freezes.* MAX *stops what he is doing.*

Keep going Max.

MAX *is frozen with fear.* WATCHER *enters.*

WATCHER: He can't keep going because he doesn't have what it takes. Poor Max Goodart. When the pressure is on, he melts. Always struggling to keep up. Consistently below the mean. It's over Max.

SAM: Don't listen Max.

WATCHER: Your little friend Mixie is gone.

MAX *starts to slump.*

And it's all your fault. You just left her there.

SAM: Max!

WATCHER: Left her there to fend for herself? What sort of friend does that?

MAX *is starting to shrink into himself.*

SAM: What would Mixie say if she was here Max?

Suddenly, MIXIE *appears. She grabs the weapon and pushes the* REGULATOR *into the paralysis zone. He is caught like a fly in a web.* MIXIE *points the weapon at* WATCHER.

MIXIE: Mixie would say: You don't know the first thing about Max. Because Max Goodart is about to finish you for good. Finish it Max!!

The sound of the menacing whisper is mixed with MAX'*s speedy fingers on the virtual keyboard. Zombie-like* STUDENTS *approach, drones whirr.* MIXIE *and* SAM *fight off the* STUDENTS *as* MAX *finishes the code. The sound is now deafening. An explosion is heard. The lights flash and fade to black. Silence. Then ... the* STUDENTS *are now without glasses; they have returned to normal.* HAMILTON *enters.* SAM *points a weapon at her.*

SAM: Who are you?

MAX *runs to the stranger.*

MAX: It's Hamilton.

HAMILTON: Max? Mixie? You found it? You found the code! I knew you would work it out.

MIXIE *draws* SAM *into view.*

MIXIE: Not without Sam. This is Sam Turing.

HAMILTON: You did this, Sam?

SAM: Max found your code in the music and the spelling error.

HAMILTON: Max, I am so proud of you.

SAM: And Mixie has been searching everywhere—

They all share a moment. Then HAMILTON *looks back to* SAM.

HAMILTON: Looks like you've made some great friends, Sam.

Beat.

But where's Toby?

TOBY *walks in.* MIXIE *and* MAX *run to her and greet* TOBY *in their own way.* TOBY *looks at* SAM.

SAM: Glad to see you back.

TOBY: Me too.

They bump shoulders and we can see that this will be the start of a strong friendship. TOBY *looks over and sees* HAMILTON. *They greet each other and start to help the other* STUDENTS *up.*

MIXIE: Come on Sam! It's time to meet the real kids at this school. This is—

All of the STUDENTS *have returned to how they were before being 'aligned'. A noisy reunion. Scenes of celebration.* MIXIE *introduces everyone to* SAM. *They all depart except for* HAMILTON *who lingers. The whispering establishes,* HAMILTON *leaves. The whispers intensify as the* REGULATORS *left on stage suddenly sit upright. The lights fade and we are left with the menacing whisper and a crackling sound. The next battle is still to come.*

THE END